Mental Health
to
Mental Wealth

i

A. N. SMITH

A FOREWORD FROM SMITH COUNSELLING & COACHING

If we are all lucky enough, we will find something that we are passionate about.

Having spent at least two days a week since the age of 8 dedicated to rugby, I was lucky enough to have found my love early. The professionalism of rugby has blessed people all over the world with the ability to enjoy a life devoted to the game they love. So, it was fitting at the tender age of 25 that I realised in my life so far, I had spent most of it playing, or watching, the sport of rugby. This led me to be reflective and to ask myself: Is there anything more I can give back when I eventually finish playing? Is there anything it has given me?

Luckily, during my sporting journey I was fortunate enough to have the opportunity to complete a BSc and MSc in Psychology and Coaching Science respectively. Granting me an extraordinary insight into the perceptions of the sporting world athletes frequently do not get due to being totally engrossed within it. Which is to some extent, fitting (arguably).

Nevertheless, as learning and research develops in the sport of rugby, athletes continue to get bigger, better, and smarter, and our dedication has done exactly the same. We have reached a point where the global game of rugby has an influence it has never seen before, following the hugely successful 2019 World Cup. But, with that great influence comes great responsibility.

Having gained a unique insight into the technical, and tactical, I believe there is a huge lag in the progress made scientifically and its conversion rate into the professional game. This prompted my founding of Smith Counselling & Coaching, which is an answer to athletes and coaches who want to further their mental scope of the game of rugby but do not know where to look.

This book aims to demonstrate that these issues can be combated through Coaching and Counselling, whilst also raising awareness on the potential issues around Mental Health in rugby. Whilst helping improve athletes understanding of critical issues such as Common Mental Disorders (CMD), this book aims to shed light on how rugby can also go one step further, and also improve athlete Mental Health AND Performance.

MENTAL HEALTH TO MENTAL WEALTH

A.N.SMITH

CONTENTS

ABBREVIATIONS

Common Mental Disorders	CMD
Continued Professional Development	CPD
Mental Health	MH
Mental Skills Training	MST
Player Development Officer	PDO
Player Welfare Manager	PWM
Rugby Football Union	RFU
Sports Counselling & Coaching	SCC
Sport Psychologist	SP
World Health Organisation	WHO

OVERVIEW

All research starts off by producing a broad statement such as: What is going on with Mental Health in Rugby?

Or, more accurately stated, all research starts off by casting out what in the long term will seem to be a large net over a mass of ambiguous concepts.

Where most interventions pose to ask questions that have been scrutinised to such a level that once hypothesised, tested, and answered, the results can be trusted up to a certain degree of accuracy. This book aims to do the opposite. Using comparable research, it aims to ask a question that once hypothesised, will only lead to answering the question of; does the question need to be asked more? and following this, how should it be answered?

So. The question:

'What is going on with Mental Health in Rugby?'

Knowing that you have dared to go deeper, as you have chosen this book, we can now begin to cipher through all the concepts and ideas that connect to this point (all things that include mental health in rugby, all things that improve mental health, things being done to help mental health, things not being done, etc.) until we get to a more succinct and more manageable question:

'What can be done in Rugby to improve how it manages the Mental Health of its Players?'

Now, having swiftly arrived at a more accurate

ix

description of what we were originally trying to ask but did not have the rigor to put as eloquently at the start of the project, we can begin.

We know athletes need more support. And, prior to most of the studies and research presented in this book, there was already significant speculation that more needs to be done, just without any real direction to go in. Divulging issues around why, and what rugby players need help and support with was a difficult task. This meant that until recently organisations were bound to meet criticism whilst they continued to employ efforts towards an unknown objective, as there was a period where the principle ideas were just extrapolated theories, from data around; 'Athlete Burnout,' 'Player Injury,' and 'Competition Stressors'.

We are now at a juncture, whereby the compiled research shows clear evidence that not only do athletes need more Mental Health (MH) support, they also need to be made more aware of the issue so they can better recognise it. As well as this, and only through research and due diligence, we find there is a strong case to make that not only is there an argument for better Mental Health (MH) facilitation, but given the scope of information and knowledge available, there is also room for professional Mental Skills Training (MST), implemented and promoted in line with the other benefits of the sport.

1
INTRODUCTION

Professionalisation of Rugby

Since the declaration by the International Rugby Board, in August 1995, that the game of rugby union would become a professional sport, rugby has undergone considerable change both on and off the field. In fact, the interest in rugby has increased exponentially with the development of International competitions such as the Heineken Cup, the Super Rugby and the Rugby World Cup (the third largest sporting event after the Olympic Games and the FIFA World Cup, attracting over two million spectators and viewed by a worldwide audience of over three billion people). The increased popularity of this sport in the last 20 years has opened new opportunities for research and stimulated the interest of sport scientists towards rugby.

Rugby is a collision sport characterised by very high physical demands. Indeed, rugby players are required to participate in frequent bouts of high intensity activity (e.g., sprinting, physical collisions, and tackles), separated by short bouts of low intensity activity (e.g., walking and jogging). Depending on playing position, the physical features of players change. Usually, forwards tend to be

1

bigger and stronger than backs, but backs tend to be faster and are the main point scorers. As a result of the high physical demands and depending on the role, rugby union requires players to have well-developed muscular strength and power, speed, agility, anaerobic and aerobic power. While the physical requirements over the maturation of rugby have become quite clear, that which involves the mental side is still not fully understood.

As Rugby has progressed research in the sport has sought to identify the skills that characterise expert performers. These studies highlighted that there is a strong indication that the performance success of high-level players is associated with specific patterns of mental proficiencies. For instance, the examined potential mental skills relevant to rugby players in the UK found traits perceived as crucial to the development of elite young rugby players were: 'Confidence', 'An Appropriate Attentional Focus', 'Game Sense', and 'Mental Toughness'. In another study, Krane & Williams (2006) tried to identify the mental skills that are related to peak performance. They found an important role of the following mental skills: 'Self-confidence, Expectations of success, Feeling in control, Focus on the present task, Viewing difficult situations as challenging and exciting, Productively perfectionistic, Positive attitudes, Cognitions about performance, and finally, Strong determination and commitment'. Similar results were also found in a study of Andrew et al., (2007) examining differences between young athletes playing at different levels.

So, what now? Given the plethora of unrefined information available, this book hopes to shed light and demonstrate that by using the knowledge not only from these pages but from the literature shared, that the benefits of continued professional development (CPD) in rugby can continue to progress the game massively, in many areas. Not only Mental Health, but also in Mental Wealth.

What is mental health?

In order to create clarity, the context in which Mental Health is being referred to must be defined. According to the World Health Organisation (WHO): "Mental health is a state of well-being in which an individual realizes his or her own abilities, can cope with the normal stresses of life, can work productively, and is able to make a contribution to his or her community."

The WHO states that emotional well-being is "something beyond the nonattendance of mental issue or inabilities." Peak mental well-being is about being self-aware and being able to comfortably operate in all the conditions that are posed to a person in everyday life, as well as taking care of one's own physical health and performance.

RUGBY INSIGHT

2
WHY RUGBY?
WHY NOW?

Where is Rugby at?

Protocol, Good practice, Rules.

Rugby is an intense sport with athletes requiring top physical, and mental conditioning to perform consistently at the highest level. The whole scope of this book is based on the hypothesis that there is an abundance of research and evidence to suggest that more could go into the game's development of the mental facets that affect a rugby player. With the optimal outcome being that players are maximising self-efficacy at both ends of the mental health the spectrum.

Many Professions outside of rugby have basic systems in place to monitor employee welfare: Appraisals systems, Feedback Loops, Exit Interviews etc. All powerful tools that empower the workforce. Now, although sport publicly is glamorised and seen as a vocation, there are those within it who are not blessed to share the same view. Studies such as that of Gouttebarge et al., (2018) state:

...a professional rugby team, typically relying on a total size of 40 players, can expect symptoms of CMD to occur among at least four players over the course of one season. (p. 1005)

A resounding statistic which can be amplified by stating that there are also those who are close to but do not qualify as sufferers who are also affected. As a performance factor, this would suggest purely from a performance perspective, upwards of roughly 10% of most squads at any time are not in their optimal operant state. Now, to address this point holistically, or rather from a 'Duty of Care' perspective, the question to ask would be: Are organisations aware of this? And do they know how to fix it?

In professional sport due to the high stakes, there is stringent management of a player's physical health. Therefore, due to the potential benefits it would also seem beneficial to examine and develop the mental side too. Not just in terms of performance, but in the interest of the player to involve mental health aspects as well. Understandably, it could be argued that the activities of an athlete, outside of their rugby career are of no concern to the companies and boards running them, but it would be naïve to state that player lifestyle does not affect player recruitment and team performance. Given this, prior to any further discussion, it must be stated whole heartedly that mental health and wellbeing should undoubtedly be a mainstay of all organisations trying to improve, moving forward.

The genuine size of rugby's MH emergency can be uncovered by revealing that today figures show that over 60% of retired players have endured issues since leaving the professional game (up to date figures available at

6

https://therpa.co.uk/). During the first 10 years after their retirement from contact team sports, former professional athletes retired from football, ice hockey, and rugby are 7–11% more likely to report symptoms of CMD with every additional sports career-related concussion. The urge to protect athletes from concussions during their career and to increase the quality of concussion management at professional sports level is at critical level, with the belief that the level of risk in the sport is and will, continue to affect the uptake of people in the sport moving forward.

The insights, incorporated by the Rugby Players' Association, have been portrayed as "a significant issue". The RPA has approached people in and around the game to build their support for retired players after its overview uncovered most of retired players had suffered various issues since leaving the game. Players did not feel in charge of their lives up to two years after they retired, and some have had monetary challenges in the initial five years post professional career. All of this information goes to show that now is the time and place for change.

Rugby Culture & Sports Psychology

Because of all the aforementioned issues, the Sports Psychologist (SP) role can take on many different roles and responsibilities within different organisations. In part, this is due to the position being what is referred to in Mellalieu (2017) as an 'outsider' position. The outsider title is given to positions and roles which are not yet ingrained in rugby culture and sometimes perceived as not necessary when compared to positions like a Head Coach, S&C (Sports & Conditioning), Video analyst, or Physiotherapist. The

Sports Psychologist (SP), Team Consultant, Player Development officer (PDO), or any other relevant title referring to professionals fulfilling the SP role is still considered a new concept in some rugby teams and cultures. Subsequently, the position is frequently personified as negative with the belief anyone seeking their guidance is suffering, or lesser than those who go without this service. This is despite successful teams such as the All Blacks having their own personal Sports Psychology Consultant (SPC) for a number of years. Help-Seeking and the use of external support systems in rugby culture is still commonly perceived as negative, or an unknown area for many athletes. Significant studies suggested that around 46% of rugby players think that specific support measures for professional rugby players were not even available to them.

Although Counselling and Coaching does take place in some teams, it is not a part of the global rugby culture. There is a huge opportunity for Regional and International Rugby organisations to employ staff to devise a way to make a SP more 'mainstream' and accessible for both teams and athletes so that the benefits can be maximised, and not just be for those 'in need'. Changing the perception of Counselling and Coaching, so that it is seen as a performance role helping players achieve their best, as well as helping players who are suffering. Boosting the profile of people using the service and also helping to convert it into an integral part of rugby culture moving forward.

3
MENTAL HEALTH

Mental Health in Rugby

It is not ground-breaking news to report that being involved in or playing group activities has been demonstrated to have many advantages to your mental health. There are numerous easily accessed web journals, articles, and reports, outlining why games from football, to hockey, to rugby, can all decidedly improve your prosperity and confidence. However, to just assume that playing professional sport, or more specifically rugby, at a high level means you are mentally 'safe' from any issues as a result of this is a disconcerting thought for the MH industry.

GREG BATEMAN - "At my worst, I found myself finding tasks needing to use up my anxious energy – like painting my garden fence at 4am and planning, reading books, listening to podcasts, writing lists, etc. Then, take more sleepers, another drink or anything so I wasn't staring at my bedroom ceiling in the dark."

Around one in every four rugby players will encounter some type of Mental Health (MH) condition every year in the UK alone. For these people, anxiety, and strains of regular day to day existence can frequently be overpowering and become an impetus that can trigger mental health issues, with the most widely recognised being depression and nervousness.

The rugby way of life to many, is one of the things that makes rugby one of the most intellectually satisfying and genuinely extraordinary games played today. To quote a referenceable moment from 'Rugby Pass,' a popular media outlet for rugby, Leicester Tigers club skipper, Tom Youngs: "Individuals state that it is just a game however this sport is more to me than that and it has been for quite a while. It's helped me through some extremely intense occasions." Any game that can bring out a sentiment of this magnitude is a sport that can undoubtedly be an overall net benefit for all involved. The social aspect and brotherhood go a long way past the 80 minutes spent on the pitch. It is for this reason that in a game where players are regularly seen as and thought to be 'alpha males', the residual effects that can arise as a result of some of the weaker aspects of the sport can begin to outweigh the benefits for some individuals. The realisation that these discussions are so effective, and significant in showing that despite the belief that some athletes are viewed as indestructible, muscle-bound proficient competitors. Now reveals that in some cases looks can be deceiving. Anybody can be affected by mental health, and for younger athletes attempting to emulate the professionals, the remarkable certainty that you will come across moments of self-doubt and worry is enough to promote the benefits of good MH and even Mental Skills Training (MST) moving forward.

Therefore, starting from the top, the sport of rugby (through mediums such as this book) is searching for new ways to help start the discussion around MH and urge individuals to voice any troubles they are encountering. The English Rugby Football Union (RFU) have collaborated with one of the main MH causes in England and Wales, known as 'Mind,' to give data, counsel, and direction to anybody engaged with rugby who might be managing MH issues. In terms of supporting mental health in Rugby the RFU also formed the Rugby Players Association, though given the results of studies such as Kola-Palmer et al., (2019) how much the addition of these structures has really been felt by its players is still debatable to this current date. In order to continue this journey awareness must be raised by organisations and action taken so that stigma around help seeking can be removed from the sport. Mental Health is a poignant issue that's treatment must be improved in rugby. This book promotes the idea that combining MH with MST is just one very effective avenue and service which could be used to help all the issues discussed and will be encouraged throughout.

JONO KITTO - Leicester Tigers scrum half Jono Kitto speaks openly about feeling suicidally depressed. Having hidden his feelings from the wider world, it was not until he spoke out about his family that he could begin his journey of recovery.

Rugby Careers Stressors

The average career of a professional rugby player is 6 years. Consequently, maximising the career of a player is vital to both the player and the organisations paying them. A positive example of this is the RFU supporting players with the 'The Benevolent Fund,' a fund a player can apply for to get grants on education, and learning outside of rugby while injured, or heading into retirement. As of 2011 the RFU instated the position of Player Development Officer (PDO), a role that is meant to encompass looking after player's wellbeing's during and after their playing days. In principle this is a role which is vital, but with the intent of adding value to the interpretation of this position later, it is vital to digress and state that only in the top tier of rugby in England (RFU Premiership) is this position accessible. There are three more tiers of professional & semi-professional rugby (National 1, National 2 and Championship) where no support of a similar nature is freely available. This presents two issues: The prominent issue is that this divide means that athletes of a lesser level do not have access to the facilities that others higher up do. Seemingly obvious, as with all sport there is a discrepancy in the allocation of resources, with more favourable environments being given to those at higher levels. However this is where the heart of the matter lies, as a governing board, if the RFU deems it necessary for some athletes to have access to PDO's, then what information are they using to insinuate those in the lower leagues (National 1, National 2 and Championship) do not? Amplifying the second supposition; that research found in contemporary literature suggests there is a correlation between players with higher Rugby Union career dissatisfaction and increased CMD rates. As a result of this, it would appear, those playing at a lower level would need PDO's more, than their more successful counterparts. This is a salient point as 'caregiving' as with any resource should be directed efficiently, and to put the point of care at the least accessible and also (relatively) least required location is ineffective by any means, and will be addressed in subsequent chapters.

Other indicators of increased risk of CMD are players who are suffering from injury, due to things such as pressure, and the stress it puts on an athlete's career. Rugby players are at risk of suffering from a significant amount of injuries during their career. Statistically, on average the risk of injury is still increasing year on year. In part due to rugby players increasing in size and speed since rugby turning professional, in around 1995. Unsurprisingly the professionalisation of any sport brings about many benefits to athletes, in terms of monetary incentives, and the boosting of career prospects for anyone playing. Nevertheless, to stay impartial while looking at the good, you also must be mindful of the bad. And given that, one of the consequences is the monetising of rugby, which means that it has slowly begun to move away from its more established amateur roots. This decisive transition brought about some significant changes to the lifestyles of top tier rugby players. Two major aspects of this are: The introduction of Junior Academies, and secondly, rugby becoming the primary (and often only) source of income for players. The increasing injury rate in combination with individuals who are increasingly dependent on their rugby income for sustainability, compounds the risk and stress in terms of dealing with injuries and the issues brought about with managing personal wellbeing while injured. As well as this, the increasing intensity decreases the length of what could already be considered a short career. In terms of Junior Academies, there needs to be an adjustment. The history of rugby traditionally had rugby players come from an educated background and begin the professional rugby transition through universities, or while playing rugby alongside education and work. This meant that individuals on the other side of their playing careers had a transition out of sport that had the potential to be more controlled and less of a lifestyle modification, reducing the amount of post career stressors.

As we move forward, we endeavour to learn more about where the profession of rugby will go. Requiring a drastic increase in research both prospectively and retrospectively. All the above evidence does is reinforce the need for more research to be done, as the lack of statistical data around player welfare and mental health in Rugby Union is beginning to infringe on Rugby's progression as a professional sport. In 2019 from a sample of 106 respondents, 77 professional Rugby League players in the UK completed a mental health survey.

Kola-Palmer et al., (2019) States:

> Using a cut-off score of 72 or less, suggests 45.5% of players experience symptoms of depression and anxiety disorders, while using a cut-off score of 60 or less suggests 27.3% of players experience severe symptoms of depression and anxiety disorders. This compares with 13.2% of men in the general population in England having common mental health disorders, comprising different types of depression and anxiety (McManus et al., 2016). (p.12)

The results of the Kola-Palmer et al., (2019) study revealed that there is still a clear gap, between where athlete mental health is, and where it should be in rugby, if we are using the general public as a gauge. (Kola-Palmer et al., (2019) also used other measures, such as Psychological Stress, Athletic Identity and Player Welfare; all of which if they did not explicitly test, showed evidence in support that professional rugby players suffered from Common Mental Disorders (CMD) if not equal to, more so than the general public. Although this study referred to Rugby League, combining the data with the findings available from contemporary Rugby Union statistics, it is easily extrapolated that we need to start progressing how we handle Mental Health in Rugby Union in order to prevent any further issues too.

Common Mental Disorders (CMD)

What are Common Mental Disorders or the CMD?

This term can be defined by various psychologists in different manners but for clarity and simplicity, it can be described as a range of different anxiety driven, and depression inducing disorders, that affect an individual at different times in their life, and for different lengths of time. The most accepted method used to measure some of the traits are in the five-item Mental Health Index (MHI-5) as exampled in.

Symptoms of Common Mental Disorders (CMD) i.e. anxiety, depression, distress, eating disorders, sleep disturbance, and adverse alcohol use among male professional rugby players has an average incidence rate of between 11-22% on a sample group of 333 athletes. Gouttebarge et al. (2018) found 94% of participants stated, "symptoms of CMD could negatively influence the performances of players" (Gouttebarge et al., 2018, p.1008). With mental health having such a definitive impact on performance, improving the way we develop professional rugby players' mental abilities could have an unprecedented effect on performance, consistency, and overall wellbeing.

JOHN KIRWAN - "Getting help [for depression], for someone like me who saw getting help as a weakness, was a big step. I did an awareness campaign and that first step was really difficult for me. I thought people were going to think I was mad."

CMD is very relevant to rugby players who get concussed or 'knocked out' during their games as they are more likely to encounter basic mental issue, possible biproducts of repetitive concussions in sport are increased risk of CMD symptoms (distress, anxiety, depression, sleep disturbance or substance abuse/dependence) and increased potential of neurodegenerative disease development, in particular chronic traumatic encephalopathy. A study distributed in the peer-reviewed journal The Physician and Sportsmedicine, reviewed 576 previous top-flight footballers, ice hockey and rugby players from seven European nations and South Africa (All were men younger than 50 years of age). The study showed players who had four or five 'concussions' during their professions were one and a half times more likely to report CMD symptoms than the individuals who had none, and players who had at least six were in the range of two times more likely. A study among former elite rugby players showed that the risk for depressive disorders increased with the number of sports career-related concussions. At the professional level, the rates of concussion have been consistently rising in recent years. For example, in the comprehensive annual injury surveillance data gathered in English professional rugby, reported concussion incidence has increased from 3 concussions per 1000 player hours in 2005 to 13.4 concussions per 1000 player hours in 2015 (England Professional Rugby Injury Surveillance Project, 2016).

There is a lot to be said for both concussion and CMD in terms of understanding and preventing its occurrence. But the notion that working on ones MH is a bad thing, is one that needs to be dispelled. Although negating CMD and improving MH is a major objective, one can only hope that the implications and intentions of this book do not only help to promote prevention of mental health issues, but to also promote Mental Skills Training. That being said, much more is being done than has been in the past for rugby players, with the medical support staff and players seeming to be embracing the constantly updating guidelines around concussion in rugby. As a result of this, despite not being where it could be, professional rugby can still be seen as at its pinnacle when it comes to the prevention and management of concussion specifically.

4
WHAT CAN WE DO?

Increasing 'Help seeking'

Rugby is a 'man's game.'

From junior level, and throughout adulthood, players are placed into competitive sporting spaces that are used to construct their identities and influence their behaviours to align with orthodox perspectives of masculine embodiment and expression. Given this, generally speaking, traditional rugby culture and being successful in the sport comes with an image of being tough, and showing no 'soft' emotions, with empirical evidence reinforcing that athletes have a self-perception that leans towards being 'tough' and adopting a 'culture of risk'. As practitioners, we want to promote mental health and deliver Counselling and Coaching that develops an athlete's mental state so that they can perform at the highest levels possible. In terms of optimal performance, research suggests when athletes present high scores in mental traits such as 'Toughness' and 'Hardiness' they are more inclined to be successful performers in the sport of rugby. Ergo, the traits and attitudes which are a catalyst for successful rugby players, do not generally speaking conform with the attitudes and behaviours of someone who is 'help-seeking'. A predicament which is evident in most studies which attempt to collect data from elite

Rugby players, with athletes reporting issues such as a lack of knowledge, or access to Counselling and Coaching like services.

Ultimately, a large issue is that athletes under use mental health services. The stigma attached to help seeking, is that of weakness and the risk of being undermined in a highly competitive sport where any edge can be advantageous. So much so that collision sports such as rugby have a tradition of athletes who 'hide' signs of weakness or 'calls for help'. Therefore, the aim here is to create and promote a learning that is aimed to encourage the use of mental health services but also, not punish 'percieved' weakness. There is still a case to be had for systems that inherently promote those who do not need help or support, but that discussion can be held another time.

KEARNAN MYALL - "You don't want other people to know you're struggling. It comes across as weakness. Was that innately programmed into me? I just thought that if I mentioned the problems I was having I wasn't going to get picked. Then I wouldn't get another contract and it would all get worse."

Undoubtedly, rugby suffers from it being an industry that, relative to other major sports is quite young in its professional age (turning professional in 1995). This means that whilst it has been possible to infer and introduce Counselling and Coaching services to rugby, arguably, it has not been an option financially to most of its potential clients for that long. Given this, it could be argued that culturally, and contextually, this is why the application of a SP is still developing, with the best way to deliver the service still being established.

An example of this is that the Rugby Football League (RFL), in recognition of the need for welfare support, introduced player welfare managers (PWM: aka. 'PDO') to all Super League clubs in 2011. The PWMs reported that they believed they have been an important resource for players, independent of the club and coaches, which has allowed players to seek support for a range of issues they might not have prior to their implementation. Furthermore, it is believed that the use of the services such as those provided by PWMs has increased over time. This is thought to be in part due to a change of culture within the sport. The PWMs felt the head coach, along with the backing of the club, and the RFL structure were important in the services being accessible and accepted. However, since the results of this and other studies were made accessible to the RFL, large-scale changes to welfare provision have been made, including making the PWMs' posts full-time. This is seen as an important contribution and commitment to players' welfare needs.

This was followed in April 2017 by the UK Government who put forward the case for increased athlete care and suggested the safety, well-being and welfare of athletes, of all ages, should be at the centre of what sport does, Winning medals is of course, really important, but should not be at the expense of the Duty of

Care towards athletes, coaches and others involved in the system'.

Career Transitions

Career transitions, whether through retirement at the end of a career or a sudden loss in career (non-normative transition) through injury or de-selection, have been the focus of numerous studies (e.g. Park et al., 2012). Studies suggest there are higher than average levels of common mental disorders (CMD) amongst rugby union players. In the rugby union study, 48% of retired players were found to be living with two or more CMD symptoms. The transition to a new career, post-sport, can be aided by education, Jennings (2015) found that educationally prepared players were better equipped for life after rugby and were able to cope with the emotional effects of retirement.

TOM JAMES - "It's like a black cloud over you. You don't want to get out of bed, you're not eating, you're not sleeping, you've got anxiety, you're not answering the phone to your best friends, you are being snappy. It got to a stage, in about 2012, where I didn't want to play rugby anymore."

Most research on welfare is concerned with supporting young athletes and their welfare needs. Whilst there are numerous studies on the welfare needs, in particular career transitions, mental health and help-seeking problems in a masculine society, there is a lack of research on how welfare needs can be supported, and best managed so to meet the athletes personal and professional needs.

Improving Mental health literacy

For the context of this study 'Mental health literacy' can be simplified to the understanding of how best to seek help, with mental health issues such as CMD, and the correct ways of handling, discussing, and preventing issues around them.

Mental health literacy is a problem that affects the RFU and its players greatly, but it must be stated that mental health literacy is a very global issue, with an increase in mental health literacy being positive anywhere it occurs. Although MH will never be the primary objective of an industry based around playing rugby. Once it becomes salient that there is an issue around something as prominent as MH, again the RFU then has a duty of care to its athletes to try to help the issue at hand. A systemic raising of awareness so that athletes can better identify between general distress, and specific work induced problems is an example of how the RFU could better facilitate players. Players being able to recognise when they are suffering, susceptible, or exposed to issues like 'burnout,' is an example of addressing problems that frequently affect mental health.

KANE PALMA-NEWPORT – It's easy to distance yourself from somebody who is suffering from mental illness, but Bath prop Kane Palma-Newport (whose family has a history of mental illness) highlights the importance of reaching out and not distancing yourself from those who are struggling.

Again, MH is a global issue, and in terms of sharing the load, help seeking does not have to just be the responsibility of the player, or the RFU. Improving MH literacy throughout organisations is a big factor, for example improving every coach's abilities to recognise, diagnose, and appropriately refer athletes that are suffering could be a pathway that has a large impact on the rugby environment culturally and literally. This is as it could not only increase help seeking, but also help in reducing the stigma around mental health by upskilling coaches and those around the people who are suffering.

Opportunity Promotion

With player injuries such as concussion becoming a much more prominent topic of discussion in mainstream media, it would get professional rugby out ahead of the curve to start planning and researching how best to implement systems that improve player wellbeing. For example, using reports to demonstrate a more educational foundation to combat any mental health literacy issues. Although on the surface, sporting industries can appear to be very mercenary and business like, it is the case that some clubs do have valuable systems in place. At Academy level, (for players not yet on professional contracts) it is possible for young athletes to engage in education and still gain qualifications alongside training. However, if you are a young athlete trying to fulfil your dream of becoming a professional rugby player it's tough to see a valiant effort being put into your revision when you are playing against your rivals at the weekend. Furthermore, for the older athletes who aren't blessed with lucrative, or long-term contracts, it is hard to place any importance on extracurricular activities such as education, when you are fighting for your place in a team.

A. N. SMITH on behalf of SMITH
COUNSELLING - "Understanding
what athletes need as people, is key
to managing player welfare.
Promoting the concept that there
are multiple ways for 'people' to
become better athletes is a major
part of successful opportunity
promotion, and what we do."

Opportunity promotion: Simple promotion of training and methods that allow individuals to build skills and habits that are not necessarily mandatory, or performance based, but rather wellbeing driven, could be an invaluable opportunity. Learning new languages, developing skills around things such as Executive Functioning, or teaching Mindfulness. There are many possibilities for athletes to prosper which do not conflict with the athlete lifestyle, even going online to get around the issues for athletes who are moving location constantly. In the interest of player wellbeing and promoting a healthy lifestyle, this is something that is easily implemented or outsourced only requiring brief conversations to gain a pivotal direction for future endeavours. A well-documented way to implement this instantly which is underused in rugby, is the 'exit interview.' Grey-Thompson (2017) states:

On leaving a recognized program in sport, as with many other professions, an independent exit interview should be carried out to understand how people feel about their experience in the sport, what could be done differently and to identify any issues that should be addressed. This interview should be administered by an independent body or players' association to ensure the sportsperson is able to be open and honest about their experience. The anonymised results should be fed back to the sport and funding body and taken into consideration to help guide future adjustments. (p.12)

This is an example of something which is not formalised in sport, and if it were, could be very beneficial. Invaluable information could be provided from athletes at various points in their careers that could potentially benefit future athletes and be the foundations of new innovations. Combining interventions such as exit interviews with prospective 'de-training' opportunities for retiring or athletes leaving a full-time environment is an opportunity to push a resource which could benefit both employer and employee massively.

The RFU's Role

As previously suggested, the RFU as an organisation can help players and teams by creating a help seeking environment which promotes and protects individuals who search for support, and answers to their problems.

Promoting and improving the roles of positions such as the PDO's, so that there is more awareness around mental health, and the benefits could go a long way to improving player welfare. As well as this, whilst not creating more work for the RFU, they could increase awareness around directing athletes to private or outsourced services. Services that specialise in working with athlete's MH help the RFU and their athletes by allowing athletes access to individuals who are specialised, and less limited in their service. An example of this is addressing the lack of

27

support for players in lower leagues. Providing or promoting services that help players address their problems is a small way the RFU could improve its care of its athletes.

The Practitioners/Experts Role

Athlete counselling is a craft that is very well established, but not very well circulated, with some athletes making the most of it and others fearing it. The difficulty for practitioners lies in providing a service that benefits everyone, as it is generally a 'one-to-one' craft. This means that although raising awareness is very beneficial. If clients are aware of other more popular services than their own, practitioners can lose out on opportunities making it a rather self-serving industry. Without deferring from the focal point, the best way practitioners can aid clients is by continuing to provide effective services and continuing to grow and adjust to the needs of the client. As previously stated, the issues many players have, is with the accessibility and the perception of the service provided by counsellors, not the service itself. It is for this reason that continuing to improve service quality, confidentiality, accessibility, and things of this nature will only better serve the RFU and the Coaching & Counselling industry moving forward.

Many sports counsellors such as Kerr (2001), have theories and practices that can be extrapolated into different sports to help athletes re-focus and adapt their mental attitudes to improve performance. However, given the depth of research into performance analysis and Strength and Conditioning (S&C) in rugby, the transfer of Mental Skills knowledge into rugby as a profession is far inferior to that of what it could be.

5
MENTAL SKILLS TRAINING (MST)

The need for Mental Skills Training

Rugby union as like any other sport has been constantly evolving over the years through law amendments and advancements in science and technology. The growth and development of the sport has led to technological advancements in the form of performance analysis (PA). This evolution of PA is ultimately aimed at improving the quality of players and team tactics in order for teams to be better than their opposition. There has been a noticeable growth in the use of PA in rugby and the amount of research focused on PA. The increase in the game's competitiveness has brought about the use of objective data as well as video footage of oppositions' performances which allows coaches to prepare for upcoming fixtures accurately and effectively.

Conversely, Psychological development is often neglected in skill development. Psychological factors should be included in talent development programs as it influences the pathways players follow to reach the elite level. Psychological skills become a determining factor of success when players possess similar skill levels and physical attributes. Competitiveness, commitment, and self-belief contribute to the on-field performance of players and the development and use of these attributes

29

should be a priority from an early age. Rugby has many versions, and one of them is Rugby Sevens, which gets its name from each team having seven players. Whilst mental preparation is key to sevens success, there appears to be a paucity of information on psychological factors in sevens. Osborne Finekaso & Treharne (2019) recently explored sources of stress (training camp, competition, and organisational stressors) experienced by professional Fijian rugby sevens players and the detrimental effects thereof. They identified a broad range of coping strategies utilised by these players in these different settings to enhance these stressors. To develop a psychological skills intervention for a specific sport or athlete the physical, technical, tactical, logistical, and psychological demands of a player should be considered (Taylor, 1995). In light of this, the aim of studies like that of Taylor (1995) was to explore the perceived psychological demands of the on and off-the-field needs of professional rugby sevens players. In-depth and context rich information was gained that could guide holistic player development within the existing talent development structures. It is research such as this that leads the direction towards a much more integrated union between Professional Rugby and Professional SP and MST.

The integration of MST can take several different routes, however for the sake of this book one individual case has been included so that real world application can be understood. There is a plethora of ways that MST can and will be applied to rugby in the future. Hopefully by demonstrating the depth of the capabilities briefly in this book, it will catalyse the industries uptake for more of its use.

Attentional skills in Rugby:

Attentional focus in sports is an example of a MST model which could be taken and applied directly from studies (Nidiffer, 1976; Nidiffer, 1992; Nideffer & Bond 2012). Attention can best be conceptualised as two broad continuums: Width (broad/narrow), and Direction (internal/external)(See Table 1.). Different situations require different levels of attentional processing for optimal performance. For example, a broad-internal focus is emphasised when analysing the game situation and planning a strategy before a scrum, while the narrow external focus is required when kicking at goal to convert a try or catching a high ball. Having the skills and knowledge of how to process certain sources of information, while omitting others is vital for successful athletes. A player is likely to receive multiple sources of information through differing continuums during a game. It is crucial to disseminate the most important information at that time, and to draw focus to them, completing the relevant tasks in the relevant moments. For example, an athlete focusing on team tactics, or spectator comments while preparing to kick at goal, as opposed to gathering information about the wind and terrain of the pitch, is not directing their attention at the appropriate stimuli. Athletes who understand and can manipulate their focus to the multiple different attentional requirements are more likely to be successful at the tasks. So, in other words, players who can rapidly modify their own attentional focus are better equipped to be elite performers, and more successful.

Table 1. Attentional Skills examples:

	NARROW	BROAD
INTERNAL	• Warm up routine • …	• Scrum • Line out • …
EXTERNAL	• Goal kicking • Catching a high ball • …	• Looking at opponent field position • …

To measure attentional skills including the attentional focus skills Nideffer developed the Test of Attentional and Interpersonal Style (TAIS: Nideffer, 1990). The use of such a device could be used in a multitude of ways for improving ability. This is just a brief example of the application of one potential facet of MST to demonstrate both the depth and breadth of potential training schemes.

Skill Differentiation

Performance Analysis (PA) is an integral part of the Rugby Profession, most notably the use of video analysis, and using different feedback systems to improve performance through inciting physical adjustments tactically or individually. The same cannot be said about athletes in terms of their mental development.

There are many aspects of an athlete's mentality that can affect performance, and it is not the case that it is the same solution for everyone in terms of optimum performance. MST with time will become a vital aspect of athlete development as there is a wealth of evidence that differentiates the elite (top level athletes) from the non-elite in terms of psychological tendencies. As the modern game begins to accept and nurture these differences it will become a matter of time until we are not just discussing factors which are generally recognised within individuals, but also selecting for, and improving them. For example, Neil et al. (2006) provides research and evidence in support of the theory that elite level athletes cope better with 'competitive anxiety' due to enhanced abilities to interpret stress, thus facilitating positive and useful thoughts, rather than debilitating ones. This focal point of development can, and is, taken into additional depth around different types of coping strategies and styles that athletes can implement to improve. However, the relevance of each individual method in the context of this book is not relevant as it is negligible to the literal application of Sport Counselling & Coaching (SCC) as a whole.

The training processes employed however, are of high significance and are what is being promoted. Continuing to use anxiety as an example, using Counselling and Coaching to help improve confidence management through mental rehearsal and self-talk, or implementing suitable relaxation strategies, are just a few examples of implementing MST in rugby. It is even the case that some sports counsellors such as Kerr (2001) claim that with time and understanding their athletes can identify predetermined mental states, and apply theory and practice (reversal theory) to personally recognise and adjust their own states. Mental development is a very intricate process as the same conditions for one athlete do not necessarily suit another. The same stressors that debilitate one athlete, may act as motivation for another. It is for this reason that although there is a plethora of research discussing how to analyse mental traits like stress, anxiety, motivation, focus etc. the only aim here is to acknowledge the benefits to learning about and improving all of them.

Team Mental States & Development

The purpose of developing mental abilities is to gain an advantage in performance through improving mental traits which affect performance. This is very beneficial on a micro level, but rugby is a team game which means that the individual parts also affect the whole (team). Team cultures and environments can be affected by the players and, more importantly, the attitudes within them. Therefore, as well as strengths, they can equally be used to identify weaknesses. Golby et al. (2003) compiled a study using 70 international Rugby League players from the 2000 Rugby League World Cup (ages 18-35, M=25.5 yr., SD=3.2), using research and information from both Mental Toughness and Hardiness. The participants of this study were categorised by factors such as where they were from and where they learnt to play. The results provided information on whether athletes' nationality influenced attributes such as their mental toughness and hardiness. The sample size of Golby et al. (2003) was limited to 70 participants and aimed to address differences that represented individuals and teams on an international scale. The study found significant differences within the sample groups, and although the overall implications of the results are questionable in terms of predictions on an international scale, the validity of the information holds accurate in terms of that specific tournament, at that present time. The results of the study suggested invoking theories such as:

> The team representing France reported comparatively higher Challenge scores than the other teams, with significantly different means from the team representing Ireland. A psychological profile high in the hardiness subscale of Challenge indicates a predisposition to view potentially difficult situations as

opportunities for personal growth and not as a threat (Maddi & Khoshaba, 2001). In the context of this present study, the French team was not expected to progress beyond the quarter-final of the competition. It would appear, therefore, that their high mean Challenge score reflected their ability to view their impending match positively as an opportunity to defeat a supposedly better team or, at the very least, to learn from the experience irrespective of the result. (Lavella, 2003, p.459)

The benefit of insight into information like this could be vital for teams, organisations, and individuals. The results from this study on the perceived 'Challenge' scores were derived from a survey used to analyse 'Hardiness'. Golby et al., (2003) used the Personal Views Survey Ill—R which provides information on a player's hardiness in terms of categories such as Commitment, Control, and Challenge. In terms of analysing performance these results were referenced post competition. If the previously referenced information was gathered pre-competition, in a methodical and informed manner, it could be the case that when used in conjunction with suitable Counselling and Coaching the information could be used to help athletes achieve the optimum operant state applicable to their ability, prior to tournaments such as the World Cup.

The depth of research published around this Psychological Performance Inventory is growing, with most studies around performance in rugby, using different scales to measure their own individually relevant psychometrics, making it difficult to judge accuracy of the Golby et al. (2003) study. The relevance of this study is that it measures psychological traits in accordance with their influence on the team, acknowledging that that SCC can greatly impact the teams' overall performance and attitudes. This type of evidence demonstrates a need for further investigations to go into teams that are perceived as successful, failing, consistent, inconsistent etc. to allow the Sports Psychology field to grow and continue to contribute knowledge in this domain.

JONNY WILKINSON - "I'd allowed that World Cup to become a defining moment, it gave me the proof I needed that I was doing everything right, so it reinforced this idea that I needed to destroy myself physically and mentally. It took a few years for the pressure to really build. And then it exploded."

Coach Training

The application of mental skills training is not limited to athletes only. Coaches seeking to improve and develop their understanding of their players and themselves could also engage in training. CPD of coaches is commonplace within sports coaching and having insight into some of the benefits of mental skills training could provide coaches with the ability to improve their players more efficiently and effectively, potentially saving them time and money. As well as this, if not even for the purpose of using the learning professionally, the extra knowledge into issues such as help-seeking and player welfare, could enable a coach to better manage their players and therefore overall team performance in the long term.

6
WHAT ARE THE LIMITATIONS?

Confirmation Bias

Mental health is a very sensitive topic as it is both subjective, and non-linear. For this reason, when researching and analysing data, to be accurate and valid you must account for conformation bias. To try to negate conformation bias in this report the types of studies investigated were actively diversified. This book tried to include and use several studies, that used a variety of methodologies, from varying standpoints on mental health in rugby. The sources were from entities who were independent and impartial such as Grey-Thompson (2017) and Kerr (2001), and also used those who were part of, or connected to rugby organisations such as Gaston (2019) and Loader (2018). This was done to try and combat conformation bias (Hart et al., 2009), and best gather a true representation of mental health in rugby today.

An inherent issue with addressing CMD and MH is the self-reported methodology of certain studies. Participants asked to recall information such as concussions and MH issues are susceptible to denial and repression as they are two defense mechanisms well-known in influencing retrospective recall of unpleasant experiences. Therefor all data of this sort is vulnerable to criticism, but it is of note that this factor does not take away from the salient points made from the results of the studies that were formed.

Scalability

Through the analysis of several studies, many opportunities have been highlighted for how rugby can improve its treatment of its athletes. Yet, very little empirical data has been referenced in combination with aspects such as cost, and time frame. Although there are many prospective ideas, it is not financially viable or efficient to implement them all at once. After the implementation of any intervention there will be a delay between the implementation and the onset of the effects. It is for this reason that improving mental health in rugby will be a gradual process, as it takes time combined with the scientific judgement and objective reasoning.

Whose Problem is Mental Health?

Large amounts of resources and research are increasingly being pushed towards helping mental health in sport, and correctly so. However, a very crucial limitation of this research is the inability to ethically know if having a form of CMD is truly always bad thing in terms of athlete 'performance'. Research such as D'urso et al., (2002) and Kerr (2001), explicitly state how some athletes prefer differing mental states during competition, such as: External Pressure, Internal Motivation, and the inhibiting or facilitating effects they produce. Consequently, even if it is generally accepted that CMD's are negative to people's everyday life by definition, conditions for people in everyday life can be very much different to, and contrary to what suits them in competition. It is for this reason that there are many successful athletes who have had mental health issues and problems away from sport, and yet they have still prospered within it. Understanding this, one limitation of this study is that; does knowing individuals can prosper with CMD's devalue the intent, and furthermore the desire, of organisations to invest in individuals who are suffering? An ethically ambiguous notion, but none the less, very relevant to the direction this research should take in terms of future involvements and investments. Attempting to drive an issue which is not paramount to your organisation's success is arguably a waste of resources? On the other hand, as practitioners, and on behalf of the athlete suffering and trying to improve mentally, this is still very much a necessity. It is because of this, that raising awareness is vital as improving research and knowledge around CMD for those who can help, will benefit everyone in the long term.

RUGBY INSIGHT

7
WHAT IS THE FUTURE OF RUGBY?

Considering the number of repetitive concussions that might occur in a rugby career, the long-term consequences vs. The long-term prospects of a rugby player, currently make rugby a very concerning sport to be involved in. Given this, the prevention of concussions should be a priority within the professional (and recreational) sport all around the country. While continued efforts at improving rugby's injury management are being promoted, preventing the occurrence of concussions (and other injuries) should be the priority in all contact sports. Especially in those sports involving high-speed collisions between players. Existing rules and regulations may have to undergo further subjugation and alterations to minimise (head) collisions, but it is undisputable that this is in the athlete's best interests, preventing any unsuitable athletes from continuing training or competing, and enforcing a conservative 'Return To Play' protocol is becoming more of a standard procedure in rugby. At the professional level in rugby, the application of concussion guidelines has been empowered and monitored by the international and national organising bodies, and rightly so.

There are many factors which could affect the implementation of MST and the Counselling and Coaching that comes with it. But it is also worthy to note that MST is a very flexible device. Limitations, such as current rugby culture, would suggest that the introduction of MST and Counselling and Coaching as a common theme within professional rugby will be a gradual process. Nevertheless, the promotion and inclusion of successful examples of them in practice will only convince more to try and imbed them in their own practice.

Positions such as PDO's have to be expanded, not only should they be prescribed with advising players, but they should able to perform duties such as informing athletes about help seeking services, and upskilled to be able to identify players that may be suffering from CMD's. There is too much evidence in support of the need to improve the Duty of Care of towards rugby players for a position like a PDO not to be maximised. Raising awareness so that athletes and coaches have better Mental Health literacy is vital. Working with coaches so they too can be a portal of information and guidance is a critical goal as this puts less emphasis on athletes to self-diagnose, whilst also reducing the fear of judgement, and scrutiny in what is already a rigorous industry.

Moving forward, more 'MST Programs at the elite level have to help promote the benefits of a SP or PDO. However as with all sport it depends greatly on one key aspect; the programs are associated with success! Accomplished teams such as the All Blacks making use of a SP gives way to conversations which allow Counselling and Coaching to be associated with success and victory, opposed to shame and failure. The natural predisposition for rugby players to be non-help seeking, having traits such as 'hardness' & 'toughness,' means the ability to change the narrative around Counselling and Coaching from one associated with negative traits to something that can help improve positive ones is very big factor. Educating athletes so they understand that MH can be worked on and seen as not just bad, but good, and very good, is a powerful catalyst in improving the uptake and perception of Counselling and Coaching in the future.

The improvements in MST is a very complex proposition in terms of developing suitable and necessary adjustments. At this point in rugby specific research, the research suggests that the main issue in improving the quality of the service is improving the uptake and awareness around the service. Examples of training programs such as SAIGE (Self talk - Arousal Control – Imagery Attention and Concentration - Goal Setting and Motivation), have been implemented successfully, and scientifically proven to demonstrate beneficial qualities which in time could be honed in and developed to suit more specific individuals or teams. The progression of rugby specific intervention at this point is only being halted by the uptake of more professional practice in sports teams.

It would be very dismissive of a lot of good research to state that counselling and Coaching needs to be drastically improved in any specific way before it is implemented more in professional teams as the research of those that do engage find most athletes feel the service is beneficial and useful already. This means that the conclusion of this information leans towards the need to improve the implementation and understanding around MST as a whole in the rugby world more so than the scientific.

JAMES HASKELL - *A firm believer that "a problem shared is a problem halved", James Haskell reveals how he boosted his confidence and self-esteem as a young player by speaking to a sports psychologist. The experience taught him how to have a positive outlook on life and gave him the tools to cope with the pressures of performing at the top level.*

8
CONCLUSION

Without more support and focus on interactions with athletes regarding their general and personal wellbeing, we will get nowhere near the root of the problem. The same way research has been a combination of independent, and governed analysis, addressing the problem appears best solved not only when the RFU raises awareness and its infrastructures, but by also outsourcing the care to independent more specialised groups. This allows the RFU not to have to carry the whole burden. There are some who prosper from having a bit of free time to work on their own endeavours. There are also those who go on to have successful and fulfilling careers after sport despite having and suffering from CMD's, nonetheless there are too many who do not. For those who lack the Executive Functioning Skills to organise their time in such a way that they can plan for a life after rugby or during rugby, these interventions are needed. Ultimately, simple measures such as showing athletes how to collate valuable experiences through their rugby careers and developing their ability to handle the professional rugby player lifestyle is key. Such that by the end of their playing years they have a solid foundation to begin in a new, or continued direction of their   choice.

9

SMITH COUNSELLING & COACHING

Mental Health in Rugby is becoming a contemporary issue with the longevity of players coming into question. None more so than from the impacts of concussion and the potential effects it may have on Mental Health. As Athletes continue to blossom into bigger and better beasts, the premise of this book was to demonstrate that the 'Rugby culture' has a duty of care not only on the pitch, but also off it! Common Mental Disorders (CMD) such as anxiety and stress are far more prevalent in rugby players than in the general public. Although all stats are the product of data above and below the norm, this books aim was to shed light that not only can players begin to fix this issue, but also become even more mentally capable.

Turning Mental Health into Mental Wealth!

This book was written to demonstrate how much more potential rugby as a profession has! Smith Counselling & Coaching is a one of a kind service. Specialised in working with athletes AND coaches in improving their understanding of the mental parameters of the sport. Working on, and off the field Smith Counselling & Coaching will not only improve performance, but also increase understanding of what it takes to be a consistent performer at the top level.

This elite service is unique in that it is for anyone, of any level, who wants to continue to improve.

If you want to learn more, simply email us at:

Smithaquile@gmail.com

Or scan the QR code below and get in contact for a **FREE** first consultation:

QUOTES

FROM THE PLAYERS EYE
(THE PART OF THE DISCUSSION TAKEN BY
WWW.RUCK.CO.UK/8-RUGBY-PLAYERS-SPEAKING-ABOUT-
DEPRESSION/)

GREG BATEMAN

"At my worst, I found myself finding tasks needing to use up my anxious energy – like painting my garden fence at 4am and planning, reading books, listening to podcasts, writing lists, etc. Then, take more sleepers, another drink or anything so I wasn't staring at my bedroom ceiling in the dark."

JAMES HASKELL

A firm believer that "a problem shared is a problem halved", James Haskell reveals how he boosted his confidence and self-esteem as a young player by speaking to a sports psychologist. The experience taught him how to have a positive outlook on life and gave him the tools to cope with the pressures of performing at the top level.

JOHN KIRWAN

"Getting help [for depression], for someone like me who saw getting help as a weakness, was a big step. I did an awareness campaign and that first step was really difficult for me. I thought people were going to think I was mad."

JONNY WILKINSON

"I'd allowed that World Cup to become a defining moment, it gave me the proof I needed that I was doing everything right, so it reinforced this idea that I needed to destroy myself physically and mentally. It took a few years for the pressure to really build. And then it exploded."

JONO KITTO Leicester Tigers scrum half Jono Kitto speaks openly about feeling suicidally depressed. Having hidden his feelings from the wider world, it was not until he spoke out about his family that he could begin his journey of recovery.

KANE PALMA-NEWPORT

It's easy to distance yourself from somebody who is suffering from mental illness, but Bath prop Kane Palma-Newport (whose family has a history of mental illness) highlights the importance of reaching out and not distancing yourself from those who are struggling.

KEARNAN MYALL

"You don't want other people to know you're struggling. It comes across as weakness. Was that innately programmed into me? I just thought that if I mentioned the problems I was having I wasn't going to get picked. Then I wouldn't get another contract and it would all get worse."

TOM JAMES

"It's like a black cloud over you. You don't want to get out of bed, you're not eating, you're not sleeping, you've got anxiety, you're not answering the phone to your best friends, you are being snappy. It got to a stage, in about 2012, where I didn't want to play rugby anymore."

Bibliography

Abram, K. M., Paskar, L. D., Washburn, J. J., & Teplin, L. A. (2008). Perceived barriers to mental health services among youths in detention. Journal of the American Academy of Child & Adolescent Psychiatry, 47(3), 301-308.

Anderson, E., & McGuire, R. (2010). Inclusive masculinity theory and the gendered politics of men's rugby. Journal of Gender Studies, 19(3), 249-261.

Andrew, M., Grobbelaar, H. W., & Potgieter, J. C. (2007). Positional differences in sport psychological skills and attributes of rugby union players. African Journal for Physical, Health Education, Recreation and Dance, 321-334.

Bampouras, M. T., Cronin, C., & Miller, K. P. (2012). Performance analytic processes in elite sport practice: An exploratory investigation of the perspectives of a sport scientist, coach and athlete. International journal of performance analysis in sport, 12(2), 468-483.

Boyd, C., Francis, K., Aisbett, D., Newnham, K., Sewell, J., Dawes, G., & Nurse, S. (2007). Australian rural adolescents' experiences of accessing psychological help for a mental health problem. Australian Journal of Rural Health, 15(3), 196-200.

Brown, J. C., Starling, L. T., Stokes, K., Viviers, P., Jordaan, E., Surmon, S., & Derman, E. W. (2019). High concussion rate in student community rugby union players during the 2018 season: implications for future research directions. Frontiers in human neuroscience, 13.

Crosier, M., Scott, J., & Steinfeld, B. (2012). Improving satisfaction in patients receiving mental health care: a case study. The journal of behavioral health services & research, 39(1), 42-54.

D'urso, V., Petrosso, A., & Robazza, C. (2002). Emotions, perceived qualities, and performance of rugby players. The Sport Psychologist, 16(2), 173-199

Davidson, D.L. & Edwards, S.D. (2014). Evaluation of a mental skills training programme for high school rugby players. African Journal for Physical, Health Education, Recreation and Dance, 20(2:1), 511-529.

Decq, P., Gault, N., Blandeau, M., Kerdraon, T., Berkal, M., ElHelou, A., ... & Peyrin, J. C. (2016). Long-term consequences of recurrent sports concussion. Acta neurochirurgica, 158(2), 289-300

Eubank, M., Nesti, M., & Cruickshank, A. (2014). Understanding high performance sport environments: Impact for the professional training and supervision of sport psychologists. Sport Exer Psychol Rev, 10, 30-7.

Fernandez-Echeverria, C., Mesquita, I., González-Silva, J., Claver, F., & Moreno, M. P. (2017). Match analysis within the coaching process: a critical tool to improve coach efficacy. International Journal of Performance Analysis in Sport, 17(1-2), 149-163.

Finekaso, G. O., & Treharne, G. J. (2018). Stress and coping in Fijian rakavi (rugby) sevens players. Sport in Society.

Fletcher, D., & Hanton, S. (2001). The relationship between psychological skills usage and competitive anxiety responses. Psychology of sport and exercise, 2(2), 89-101.Gaston, L. E. (2019). The Quad-Lemma: how the Rugby Players Association Benevolent Fund was establish to address the welfare needs in the professional format of rugby union. Sport in Society, 22(3), 462-475.

Gilbourne, D., & Richardson, D. (2006). Tales from the field: Personal reflections on the provision of psychological support in professional soccer. Psychology of sport and exercise, 7(3), 325-337.

Golby, J., Sheard, M., & Lavallee, D. (2003). A cognitive-behavioral analysis of mental toughness in national rugby league football teams. Perceptual and Motor skills, 96, 455-462.

Goldberg, D. P., & Huxley, P. (1992). Common mental disorders: a bio-social model. Tavistock/Routledge.

Gorely, T., Lavallee, D., Bruce, D., Teale, B. C., & Lavallee, R. (2001). A sampling of perceptions of potential users of the Australian Athlete Career and Education program. Academic Athletic Journal, 15, 11-21.

Gouttebarge, V., Hopley, P., Kerkhoffs, G., Verhagen, E., Viljoen, W., Wylleman, P., & Lambert, M. (2018). A 12-month prospective cohort study of symptoms of common mental disorders among professional rugby players. European journal of sport science, 18(7), 1004-1012.

Gouttebarge, V., Hopley, P., Kerkhoffs, G., Verhagen, E., Viljoen, W., Wylleman, P., & Lambert, M. I. (2017). Symptoms of common mental disorders in professional rugby: an international observational descriptive study. International journal of sports medicine, 38(11), 864-870.

Gouttebarge, V., Kerkhoffs, G., & Lambert, M. (2016). Prevalence and determinants of symptoms of common mental disorders in retired professional Rugby Union players. European journal of sport science, 16(5), 595-602.

Green, M., Morgan, G., & Manley, A. (2012). Elite rugby league players' attitudes towards sport psychology consulting. Sport & Exercise Psychology Review, 8(1), 32-44.

Grey-Thompson, T. (2017). Duty of care in sport. Independent report to the Government. Accessed August, 2, 2017.

Grobbelaar, H. W. (2018). Effects of a psychological skills training programme for underserved Rugby Union players. South African Journal for Research in Sport, Physical Education and Recreation, 40(1), 39-53.

Gulliver, A., Griffiths, K. M., & Christensen, H. (2012). Barriers and facilitators to mental health help-seeking for young elite athletes: a qualitative study. BMC psychiatry, 12(1), 157.

Hanton, S., Mellalieu, S. D., & Hall, R. (2004). Self-confidence and anxiety interpretation: A qualitative investigation. Psychology of sport and exercise, 5(4), 477-495.

Hart, W., Albarracín, D., Eagly, A. H., Brechan, I., Lindberg, M. J., & Merrill, L. (2009). Feeling validated versus being correct: a meta-analysis of selective exposure to information. Psychological bulletin, 135(4), 555.

Holland, M. J., Woodcock, C., Cumming, J., & Duda, J. L. (2010). Mental qualities and employed mental techniques of young elite team sport athletes. Journal of clinical sport psychology, 4(1), 19-38.

Impaired, Community-Dwelling Elderly Patient. Retrieved from. https://pubmed.ncbi.nlm.nih.gov/16274382/ 13/07/2020

Jacobson E. Denial and repression. J Am Psychoanal Assoc. 1957;5:61–92.

Jennings, S. (2015). Are educationally prepared rugby players better equipped to enter the transition process and into life after rugby? (Doctoral dissertation, Dublin Business School).

Kamm, R. L. (2005). Interviewing principles for the psychiatrically aware sports medicine physician. Clinics in sports medicine, 24(4), 745-769.

Kerr, J. H. (2001). Counselling athletes: Applying reversal theory. Psychology Press.

Kobasa, S. C. (1979). Stressful life events, personality, and health: an inquiry into hardiness. Journal of personality and social psychology, 37(1), 1.

Kola-Palmer, S., Buckley, S., Kingston, G., Stephen, J., Rodriguez, A., Sherretts, N., & Lewis, K. (2019). "Someone to Talk to": Influence of Player Welfare Provision on Mental Health in Professional Rugby League Players. Journal of Clinical Sport Psychology, 13(3), 486-503.

Krane, V., & Williams, J.M. (2006). Psychological characteristics of peak performance. In J.M. Williams (Ed.), Applied sport psychology: Personal growth to peak performance (5th ed., pp. 207–227). New York: McGraw-Hill.

Krueger, R. F. (1999). The structure of common mental disorders. Archives of general psychiatry, 56(10), 921-926.

Kruyt, N., & Grobbelaar, H. (2019). Psychological demands of international rugby sevens and well-being needs of elite South African players. Frontiers in psychology, 10, 676.

Larkin, D., Levy, A., Marchant, D., & Colin, M. (2017). When winners need help: Mental health in elite sport. The Psychologist, 30, 42-47.

Lavallee, D. (2006). Career awareness, career planning, and career transition needs among sports coaches. Journal of Career Development, 33(1), 66-79.

Levy, Andrew R., Remco CJ Polman, Peter J. Clough, David C. Marchant, and Keith Earle. "Mental toughness as a determinant of beliefs, pain, and adherence in sport injury rehabilitation." Journal of Sport Rehabilitation 15, no. 3 (2006): 245-254.

Lewis, K., Rodriguez, A., Kola, S., & Sherretts, N. (2016). Mental health and rugby football league: is enough being done to support players?. Journal of Sports Sciences, 34(sup1), i-s85.

Lewis, K., Rodriguez, A., Kola-Palmer, S., & Sherretts, N. (2018). 'It's not mind blowing really.... it's about keeping people happy': the perceptions of player welfare managers in Rugby Super League. Qualitative Research in Sport, Exercise and Health, 10(5), 635-654.

Linder, D. E., Brewer, B. W., Van Raalte, J. L., & De Lange, N. (1991). A negative halo for athletes who consult sport psychologists: Replication and extension. Journal of Sport and Exercise Psychology, 13(2), 133- 148.

Liston, K., Reacher, D., Smith, A., & Waddington, I. (2006). Managing pain and injury in non-elite rugby union and rugby league: A case study of players at a British university. Sport in Society, 9(3), 388-402

Loader, J. S. J. (2018). The impact of mental health campaigns on attitudes and help-seeking behaviours in New Zealand rugby union players.

Loehr, J. E. (1986). Mental toughness training for sports: Achieving athletic excellence (p. 216). S. Greene Press.

Maddi, S. R., & Khoshaba, D. M. (2001). Personal views survey. Hardiness Institute.

Maddi, S. R., & Khoshaba, D. M. (2003). Hardiness training for resiliency and leadership. Promoting capabilities to manage posttraumatic stress: Perspectives on resilience, 43-58.

McKee, A. C., Cairns, N. J., Dickson, D. W., Folkerth, R. D., Keene, C. D., Litvan, I., ... & Tripodis, Y. (2016). The first NINDS/NIBIB consensus meeting to define neuropathological criteria for the diagnosis of chronic traumatic encephalopathy. Acta neuropathologica, 131(1), 75-86.

McManus, S., Bebbington, P., Jenkins, R., & Brugha, T. (2016). Mental health and wellbeing in England: Adult Psychiatric Morbidity Survey 2014. A survey carried out for NHS Digital by NatCen Social Research and the Department of Health Sciences, University of Leicester.

Meisner, K. (2015). A Theory of Men's Help-Seeking from Informal Others for Mental Wellbeing Problems.

Mellalieu, S. D. (2017). Sport psychology consulting in professional rugby union in the United Kingdom. Journal of Sport Psychology in Action, 8(2), 109-120.

Mental Health overview (2020) Retrieved from www.who.com 13/07/2020

Mental health: strengthening our response. (2018) Retrieved from https://www.who.int/news-room/fact-sheets/detail/mental-health-strengthening-our-response 13/07/2020

Morgan, P. B., Fletcher, D., & Sarkar, M. (2015). Understanding team resilience in the world's best athletes: A case study of a rugby union World Cup winning team. Psychology of sport and exercise, 16, 91- 100.

Neil, R., Mellalieu, S. D., & Hanton, S. (2006). Psychological skills usage and the competitive anxiety response as a function of skill level in rugby union. Journal of sports science & medicine, 5(3), 415.

Nideffer, R. (1993). Attention control training. In R. N. Singer, M. Murphey, & I. K. Tennant (Eds.), Handbook of research on sport psychology (pp. 127–170). New York: Macmillan.

Nideffer, R. M. (1990). Use of the Test of Attentional and Interpersonal Style (TAIS) in sport. The Sport Psychologist, 4(3), 285–300.

Nideffer, R. M., & Bond, J. (2012). A cross cultural examination of the concentration skills of elite level athletes

O'Donoghue, P., Ball, D., Eustace, J., McFarlan, B., & Nisotaki, M. (2016). Predictive models of the 2015 Rugby World Cup: accuracy and application. International Journal of Computer Science in Sport, 15(1), 37-58.

Ong, N. C., & Griva, K. (2017). The effect of mental skills training on competitive anxiety in schoolboy rugby players. International Journal of Sport and Exercise Psychology, 15(5), 475-487.

Ramaeker, J., & Petrie, T. A. (2019). "Man up!": Exploring intersections of sport participation, masculinity, psychological distress, and help-seeking attitudes and intentions. Psychology of Men & Masculinities, 20(4), 515.

Reardon, C. L., & Factor, R. M. (2010). Sport psychiatry. Sports Medicine, 40(11), 961-980.

Roberts, S., & Lavallee, D. (2004). A developmental perspective on transitions faced by athletes. Developmental sport and exercise psychology: A lifespan perspective, 507-527.

Roberts, S., & Stokes, K. (2017). RFU Community Rugby Injury Surveillance and Prevention Project CRISP Season Report 2016-2017.

Samuel, R. D., & Tenenbaum, G. (2011). The role of change in athletes' careers: A scheme of change for sport psychology practice. The Sport Psychologist, 25(2), 233-252.

Sharp, L. A., Woodcock, C., Holland, M. J., Cumming, J., & Duda, J. L. (2013). A qualitative evaluation of the effectiveness of a mental skills training program for youth athletes. The Sport Psychologist, 27(3), 219-232.

Sheard, M. (2009). A cross-national analysis of mental toughness and hardiness in elite university rugby league teams. Perceptual and motor skills, 109(1), 213-223.

Sheard, M., Golby, J., & Van Wersch, A. (2009). Progress toward construct validation of the Sports Mental Toughness Questionnaire (SMTQ). European Journal of Psychological Assessment, 25(3), 186-193.

Souter, G., Lewis, R., & Serrant, L. (2018). Men, mental health and elite sport: A narrative review. Sports medicine-open, 4(1), 57.

Taylor, J. (1995). A conceptual model for integrating athletes' needs and sport demands in the development of competitive mental preparation strategies. The Sport Psychologist, 9, 339–357.

Topp C.W., Østergaard S.D., Søndergaard S., & Bech P. (2015). The WHO-5 Well-Being Index: A Systematic Review of the Literature.

Vahed, Y., Kraak, W., & Venter, R. (2016). Changes on the match profile of the South African Currie Cup tournament during 2007 and 2013. International Journal of Sports Science & Coaching, 11(1), 85-97.

Wadsworth, N., Paszkowec, B., & Eubank, M. (2020). One-to-One Support With a Professional Rugby League Player: A Case for Referral?. Case Studies in Sport and Exercise Psychology, 4(S1), S1-1.

Ware Jr, J. E., & Sherbourne, C. D. (1992). The MOS 36-item short-form health survey (SF-36): I. Conceptual framework and item selection. Medical care, 473-483.

Watson, J. C. (2006). Student-athletes and counseling: Factors influencing the decision to seek counseling services. College Student Journal, 40(1).

What   is   mental   health   (2020)   Retrieved   from https://www.medicalnewstoday.com/articles/154543 13/07/2020

WHO. (1998). Wellbeing Measures in Primary Health Care/The Depcare Project. WHO Regional Office for Europe: Copenhagen.

Williams, S., Trewartha, G., Kemp, S., Brooks, J., Fuller, C., Taylor, A., ... & Stokes, K. (2017). HOW MUCH RUGBY IS TOO MUCH? A SEVEN-SEASON PROSPECTIVE COHORT STUDY OF MATCH EXPOSURE IN [PROFESSIONAL RUGBY UNION PLAYERS. British Journal of Sports Medicine, 51(4), 410-410.

Wright, C., Atkins, S., & Jones, B. (2012). An analysis of elite coaches' engagement with performance analysis services (match, notational analysis and technique analysis). International Journal of Performance Analysis in Sport, 12(2), 436-451.

Wylleman, P., & Lavallee, D. (2004). A developmental perspective on transitions faced by athletes. Developmental sport and exercise psychology: A lifespan perspective, 507-527.